WORLD'S WEIRDEST
SEA CREATURES

by M.L. Roberts

Troll Associates

WELCOME TO MY NIGHTMARE

THE WOLF FISH

This is one scary-looking fish! Its powerful jaws and sharp teeth are deadly weapons, and the wolf fish isn't afraid to use them. It can crush the shells of crabs, and it will also attack fishermen who are unlucky enough to catch it in their nets. A wolf fish's bite is extremely painful, and it can even crush a person's finger in its deadly jaws.

Wolf fish live in the cool waters of the North Atlantic Ocean. They grow to about 3 feet (1 m) long.

A wolf fish may be nasty, but it can also be useful to people. Its tough skin can be made into leather and used for pouches, bookbindings, and more. And this tasty fish is a favorite food in Iceland.

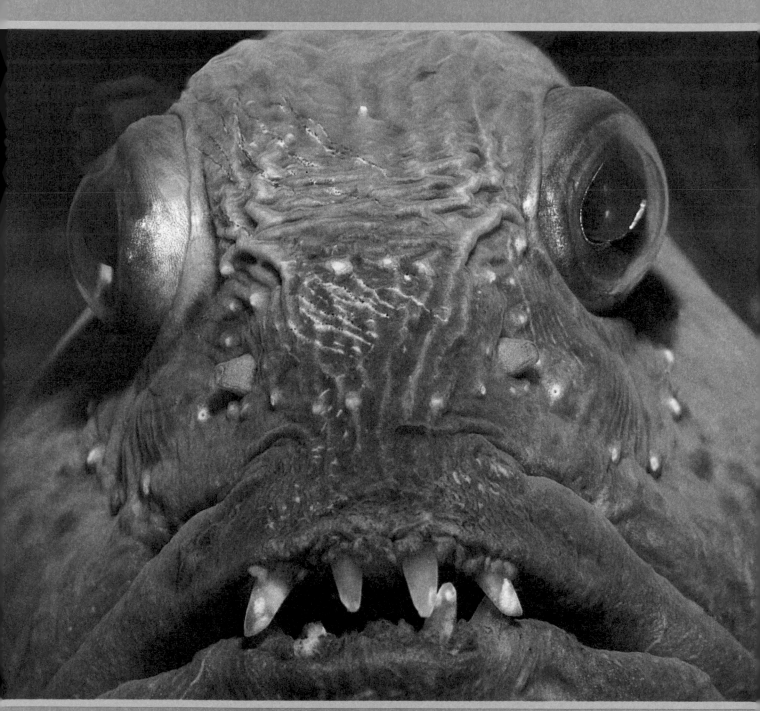

GO FISH!

THE ANGLERFISH

People aren't the only ones who like to go fishing. The anglerfish has a natural fishing pole — a special fin growing out of its head. A glowing blob of "bait," called the *esca*, dangles from the end of the pole. Passing fish often mistake the twitching esca for a worm or shrimp and come closer for a bite. But it's the anglerfish that does the biting — opening its mouth and gobbling up the other fish.

In most species of anglerfish, the male doesn't have the special fish-catching fin. It has to rely on the female to find food. The male bites the female's body and hangs on for the rest of his life. If the male does not find a female to hang onto, he will die in a few months!

An anglerfish's stomach can stretch to a very large size. That means it can snack on fish, squid, and deep-sea crabs, all of which are much larger than the anglerfish is. This is one animal whose eyes aren't bigger than its stomach!

NO BONES ABOUT IT

THE SQUID

quids are part of a family called *mollusks*. Mollusks have no bones. Instead, their bodies are protected by a shell. A squid's shell is *inside* its body.

A squid doesn't swim like ordinary animals do. It's jet-propelled! The squid fills folds in its body with water, then shoots it out through a special tube beneath its head. This helps the squid make a speedy getaway from predators. A squid can also squirt a cloud of ink into the water to hide from other animals. And, if all else fails, the squid can just try to blend in. Its body can change color to match the rocks and sand around it.

Squids have ten arms, which are covered with sucking disks. The squid uses its arms to catch fish. Then it chews them up with its powerful jaws — and its tooth-covered tongue!

WAY DOWN AT THE BOTTOM OF THE SEA

THE SKATE

This creature looks like a large, flat disk as it cruises along the sandy bottom, looking for fish, snails, and clams to eat. Its thin tail acts like a rudder and also contains electric organs that help the skate find its prey. The skate sucks in food through a tube on the front of its head. It's kind of like an underwater vacuum cleaner!

Skates can grow up to 6½ feet (2 m) long, and weigh up to 100 pounds (45 kg). Their skeletons are made of *cartilage* (the same bendable material inside a person's nose), not bone.

Skates lay their eggs in cases at the bottom of the sea. Long ago, people found these cases and thought they were left in the water by mermaids. Even today, a skate's egg cases are sometimes called *mermaids' purses!*

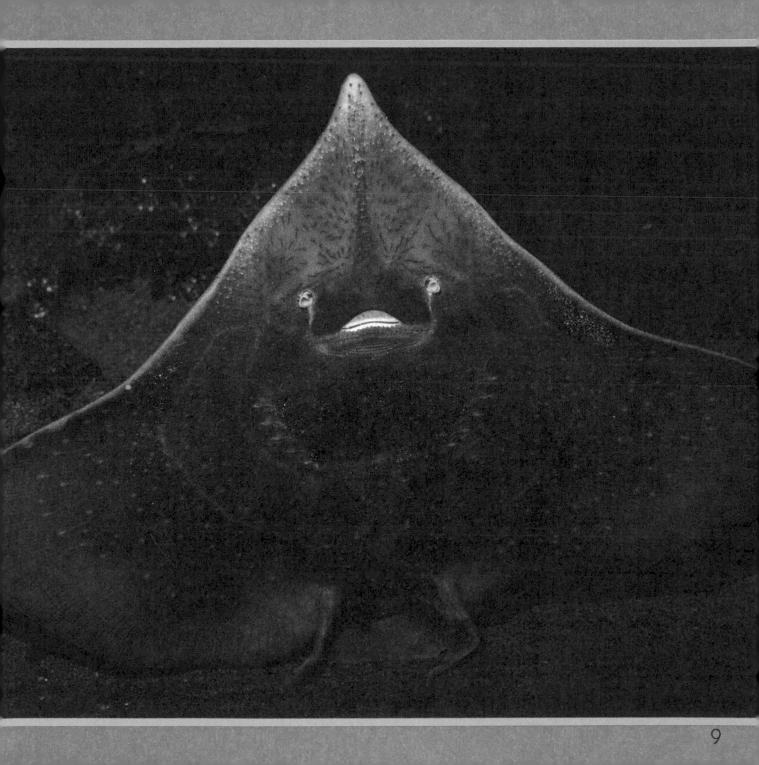

PREDATOR
OF THE DEEP

THE WHITETIP REEF SHARK

harks have a bad reputation as vicious, people-eating, killing machines. While the whitetip reef shark is very dangerous to other fish, you'll be glad to know it doesn't usually attack people.

Sharks have incredible senses of taste and vibration. A whitetip shark can sense even tiny amounts of blood in the water, and it can pick up vibrations many miles away. These sharp senses help the shark locate injured fish and move in for the kill.

Whitetip sharks live around coral caves in reefs. They like to keep warm, so you can usually find them swimming in the tropical waters of the Pacific Ocean.

A shark's body is very simple. Its skeleton is made of cartilage, not bone. It doesn't even have gills, as most fish do, just simple "gill slits" on the sides of its head. But it must be doing something right — the shark has been king of the ocean for millions of years!

11

ARMED AND READY

THE LOBSTER

Imagine wearing a suit of armor every day of your life. The lobster does! Its stiff shell doesn't grow along with its body, so every once in a while, the lobster crawls out of its shell and grows a new one. During its first year, the lobster may shed its shell as many as 7 times!

Lobsters can't see, hear, or smell very well. So how do they find out what's going on around them? Their shells are covered with thousands of hairlike bristles. These bristles can sense the slightest movement in the water and keep the lobster in touch with the world.

A female lobster can give birth to up to 90,000 babies at a time! It's a good thing Mom has so many babies, because most lobsters are eaten by fish and other lobsters before they're a year old.

Did you know that a lobster can be right- or left-handed, just like a person? A lobster's 2 front claws are not the same size. If a lobster's heavy claw is on the right side, we say it is right-handed.

WALKING ON STILTS

THE ARROW CRAB

Hey Mr. Crab, what long legs you have! The arrow crab's thin legs help it scuttle along the ground when it's looking for food or running away from an enemy. A crab's legs are covered with an armorlike shell. But the shell is jointed, so the creature can move around easily.

Crabs are part of a family called *crustaceans*. There are about 4,500 different kinds of crabs. Some live along the shoreline, while others prefer to swim in deep water. Crabs like to eat other small crustaceans. And many animals — and people — like to eat crabs!

Some crabs don't have shells of their own, so they have to move into shells left by other animals. If the hermit crab finds a shell that's still occupied, it will kill the owner and move right in. Talk about a bad neighbor!

"THE TIGER OF THE SEA"
THE GREAT BARRACUDA

This fish has a pretty tough nickname, and it deserves it! The barracuda is fast and fearless, and its powerful jaws are full of sharp teeth. Barracudas can swim incredibly fast as they sneak up on schools of fish and devour them. This fish has also been known to attack people!

The great barracuda can grow up to 6 feet (1.8 m) long. Its home is the Atlantic Ocean from the southeastern United States to Brazil. The great barracuda lives in shallow water, but it swims far out into the ocean, too.

Some barracudas live in the tropical waters of the Pacific, where there are lots of coral reefs. If a barracuda eats a poisonous coral and then is eaten by a person, that person can die. So you'd better pass if you're ever offered a barracuda casserole!

BEWARE OF THE BLOB

THE JELLYFISH

Some people worry about sharks when they go to the beach, but the animal to *really* watch out for is the innocent-looking jellyfish. If you touch one of these animals, you can get a nasty sting.

A jellyfish's mouth is located under its body, and long tentacles hang down around it. These tentacles have stingers that send out hooked threads to catch small fish, shrimp, and crabs. A poison in these threads paralyzes the prey and makes it easier to drag into the jellyfish's mouth.

A jellyfish swims by puffing open its body, then quickly pulling it closed. This squeezes water out from under the body and forces the jellyfish upward. When a jellyfish stops moving, it sinks!

Most jellyfish can give you a nasty sting, but some can even kill you! The sea wasp, a type of jellyfish found off the coast of Australia, kills more people per year than sharks do. Its poison is so deadly, people have died less than 3 minutes after being stung!

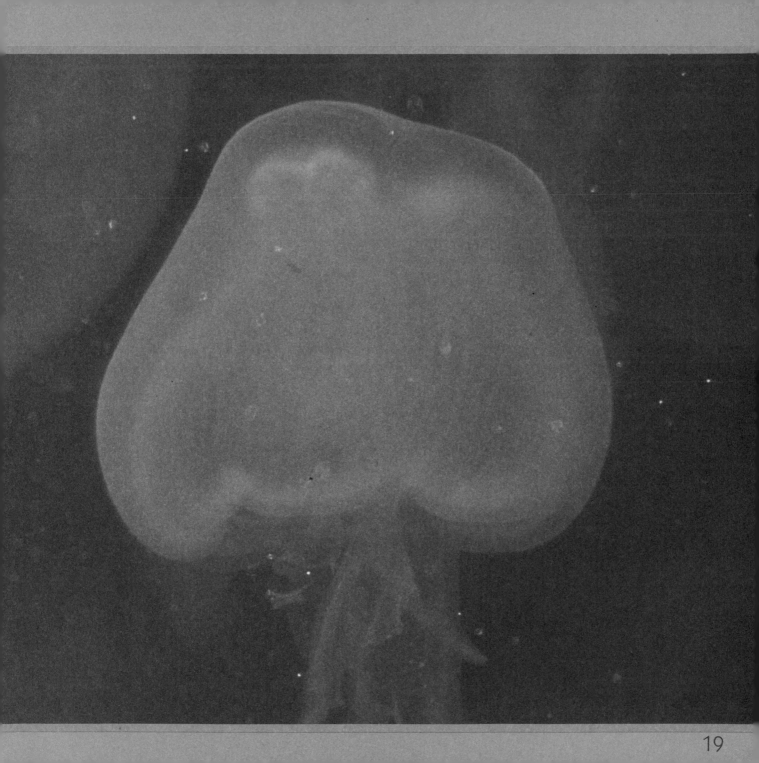

RIDE 'EM, FISH!

THE SEA HORSE

The sea horse is actually a fish, but it certainly is easy to see how it got its name! This tiny creature is usually less than 6 inches (15 cm) long. It eats tiny crustaceans by sucking them into its mouth.

Most sea animals use their tails to help them swim, but the sea horse's tail serves a completely different purpose. The sea horse uses its tail to hold onto seaweed, just like a monkey uses its tail to hang from a tree branch.

In most animal species, it's the female who takes care of the eggs. Not the sea horse. The female sea horse lays her eggs in a special pouch on the male's body, and he carries the eggs until they hatch. Just call him Mr. Mom!

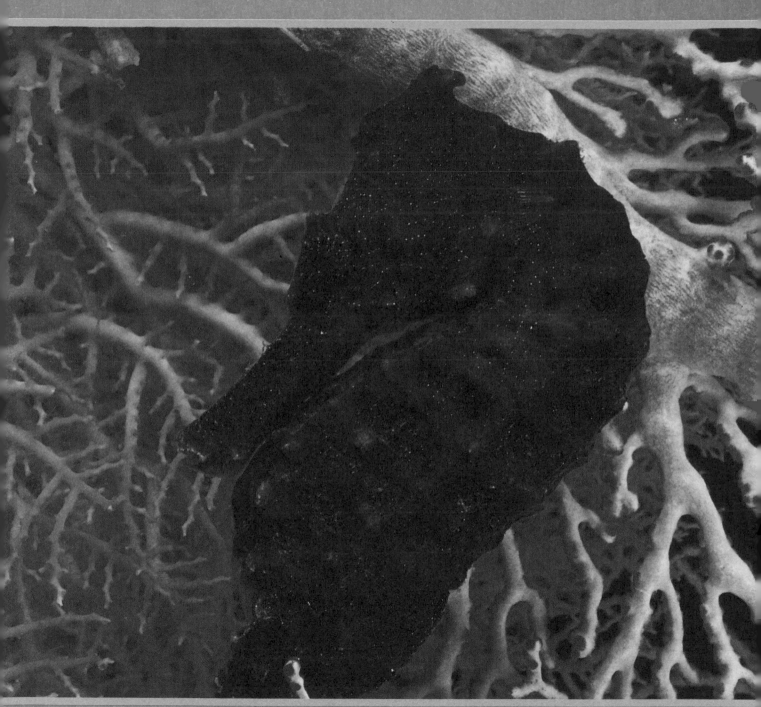

A SLITHERY SEA SERPENT

THE EEL

The eel looks like a snake, but don't let appearances fool you. It is actually a fish. There are about 600 different species of eels. Most live in the ocean, but some can live in fresh water, too.

An eel's body is covered with small scales under a slimy skin. The eel's slippery coating makes it hard to catch, and also allows it to survive out of the water. It may even help the eel swim faster.

Eels usually spend the day resting between rocks or lying buried in the sand. At night they come out to eat shrimp, crabs, fish, and other small animals.

Eels are born in the warm waters of the Sargasso Sea, which is part of the North Atlantic Ocean. Eels swim all over the world when they grow up, but the females always swim back to the Sargasso Sea to lay their eggs! Somehow, their babies find their way back to the same waters where their parents lived, even though they were never there before. How do the eels know where to go? No one really knows.

THE ELEPHANT'S COUSIN

THE MANATEE

The manatee is sometimes called the sea cow, but it is actually related to the elephant! Manatees are not fish. They are mammals, and need to come up to the surface to breathe. Like elephants, manatees eat grass — more than 100 pounds (45 kg) a day! They are the only marine mammals that eat plants, and they are the largest vegetarian in the sea.

Manatees are heavy — about 1,500 pounds (680 kg) — and they look clumsy. But water supports the manatee's body, so the animal can turn somersaults, headstands, and more. Its rounded tail makes the manatee a good swimmer.

There is no such thing as a full-grown manatee. A manatee will continue to grow as long as it lives!

Manatees and their close relative, the dugong, may be the basis for the legendary mermaid. Both manatees and dugongs stand up in the water, and often cuddle their babies against their chest. Sailors who saw these animals from a distance may have thought they were looking at a woman with the tail and flippers of a fish. It just goes to show you, you can't always believe your eyes!

FULL OF HOT AIR

THE PUFFERFISH

his fish's motto could be "the bigger, the better." When the pufferfish is threatened, it quickly swallows water or air, until it has blown its body into a large, round ball. This is usually enough to scare away most predators.

If its appearance isn't scary enough, this fish has another way to make any animal sorry it considered the puffer as a snack. The pufferfish is covered with a poisonous mucus that can kill any animal who tries to eat it.

One type of puffer, called the porcupine fish, is covered with sharp spines. When the porcupine fish inflates its body, these spines pop out. Most animals quickly decide to find something less pointy to eat!

A SPIKY FELLOW

THE SEA URCHIN

This colorful creature looks like a pretty plant, but it's actually an animal! Sea urchins are related to starfish. Their round bodies are covered with long, movable spines. Sometimes these spines are very sharp or covered with poison, so divers need to beware!

Sea urchins eat plants found on rocks and on the bottom of the sea. They scrape their food off rocks with five movable teeth found on the bottom of their bodies. Some sea urchins can even dig holes in the rocks with their teeth!

The sea urchin is not much of a traveler, but it does manage to get around. Some sea urchins move by pushing themselves along with their spines. Others have *tube feet* with tiny suckers. They use these feet to pull themselves over rocks. Even a sea urchin gets tired of being in the same place for too long!

"FEED ME!"

THE CROWN OF THORNS STARFISH

The starfish has one main purpose in life: to eat. And it doesn't waste time chewing or swallowing!

A starfish actually eats with its stomach. Its mouth, which is located in the *central disk,* or center of its body, is not big enough to take in large pieces of food. So the starfish pushes its stomach out through the mouth and digests its prey on the spot!

The crown of thorns starfish may not look particularly dangerous, but don't let that fool you! This starfish has eaten its way through coral reefs, and is causing a lot of damage to Australia's Great Barrier Reef. Divers also need to be careful — the crown of thorn's poisonous spines have killed several people.

Imagine being able to grow a new arm if one of yours was cut off! The starfish can do just that. In fact, if enough of the central disk is attached, a whole new starfish can grow from just one of its arms!

Index

Page numbers in **bold** indicate photograph.

LIBRARY OF CONGRESS CATALOGING-IN-PUBLICATION DATA

Roberts, M.L., (date)
  World's weirdest sea creatures / by M.L. Roberts.
     p.   cm.
  ISBN 0-8167-3230-2 (lib.) ISBN 0-8167-3689-8 (pbk.)
  1. Marine fauna—Juvenile literature.   [1. Marine animals.]
I. Title.
QL122.2.R63 1995
591.92—dc20   93-21053

Copyright © 1995 by Troll Associates, Inc. WhistleStop is a trademark of Troll Associates. All rights reserved. No part of this book may be used or reproduced in any manner whatsoever without written permission from the publisher.

Printed in the United States of America.
10 9 8 7 6 5 4 3

Photo credits:

All photos courtesy of Tom Stack & Associates: Photo on page 3 © by Kerry T. Givens, pages 5, 11, 21, and 31 © by Dave B. Fleetham, pages 7 and 23 © by Ed Robinson, page 9 © by Evelyn Tronca, pages 13, 15, 17, 19, 27, and 29 © by Brian Parker, page 25 © by D. Holden Bailey.

Cover photo © by Brian Parker, courtesy of Tom Stack & Associates.